SandCastle

Sight Words

# Any Day but Today!

**Kelly Doudna**

Consulting Editor Monica Marx, M.A./Reading Specialist

**ABDO**
**Publishing Company**

Published by SandCastle™, an imprint of ABDO Publishing Company, 4940 Viking Drive, Edina, Minnesota 55435.

Printed in the United States.

Credits
Edited by: Pam Price
Curriculum Coordinator: Nancy Tuminelly
Cover and Interior Design and Production: Mighty Media
Photo Credits: BananaStock Ltd., Brand X Pictures, Corbis Images, PhotoDisc

Library of Congress Cataloging-in-Publication Data

Doudna, Kelly, 1963-
     Any day but today! / Kelly Doudna.
          p. cm. -- (Sight words)
     Includes index.
     Summary: Uses simple sentences, photographs, and a brief story to introduce six different words: a, any, but, other, what, will.
     ISBN 1-59197-464-X
     1. Readers (Primary) 2. Vocabulary--Juvenile literature. [1. Reading.] I. Title. II. Series.

PE1119.D67516 2003
428.1--dc21

                                                                        2003050312

SandCastle™ books are created by a professional team of educators, reading specialists, and content developers around five essential components that include phonemic awareness, phonics, vocabulary, text comprehension, and fluency. All books are written, reviewed, and leveled for guided reading, early intervention reading, and Accelerated Reader® programs and designed for use in shared, guided, and independent reading and writing activities to support a balanced approach to literacy instruction.

## Let Us Know

After reading the book, SandCastle would like you to tell us your stories about reading. What is your favorite page? Was there something hard that you needed help with? Share the ups and downs of learning to read. We want to hear from you! To get posted on the ABDO Publishing Company Web site, send us e-mail at:

**sandcastle@abdopub.com**

SandCastle Level: Beginning

# Featured Sight Words

a        any

but        other

what        will

a

The class has a pair
of pet guinea pigs.

**any**

Rob can use any computer.

**but**

Deb eats lunch now but will go to class later.

other

Bob rides the bus with other kids.

what

Steph knows what the answer is.

will

Language class will last for an hour.

# A Day at School

Lin works on a math problem.

She wonders what the answer is.

Lin asks the other girl, but she does not know either.

Mrs. Clark will help Lin.

Lin is glad the test is any day but today.

# More Sight Words in This Book

| | |
|---|---|
| an | know |
| at | not |
| can | of |
| day | on |
| for | she |
| go | the |
| has | to |
| is | with |

All words identified as sight words in this book are from Edward Bernard Fry's "First Hundred Instant Sight Words."

# Picture Index

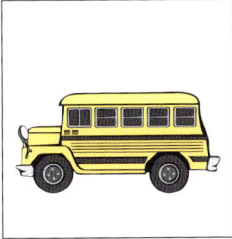

**bus,** p. 11

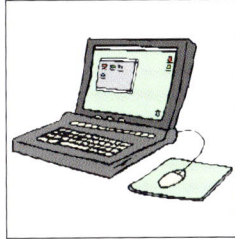

**computer,** p. 7

**girl,** p. 18

**guinea pigs,** p. 5

**kids,** p. 11

**lunch,** p. 9

23

# About SandCastle™

A professional team of educators, reading specialists, and content developers created the SandCastle™ series to support young readers as they develop reading skills and strategies and increase their general knowledge. The SandCastle™ series has four levels that correspond to early literacy development in young children. The levels are provided to help teachers and parents select the appropriate books for young readers.

**Emerging Readers**
(no flags)

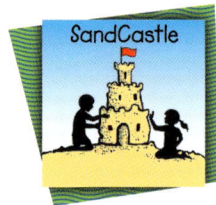

**Beginning Readers**
(1 flag)

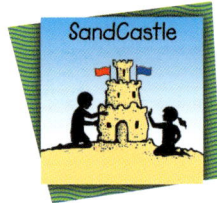

**Transitional Readers**
(2 flags)

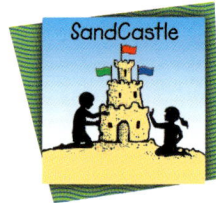

**Fluent Readers**
(3 flags)

These levels are meant only as a guide. All levels are subject to change.

**ABDO Publishing Company**

To see a complete list of SandCastle™ books and other nonfiction titles from ABDO Publishing Company, visit www.abdopub.com or contact us at:

4940 Viking Drive, Edina, Minnesota 55435 • 1-800-800-1312 • fax: 1-952-831-1632